W9-AAW-134

HOW-TO LIBRARY

LEARNING TO MAKE BOOKS

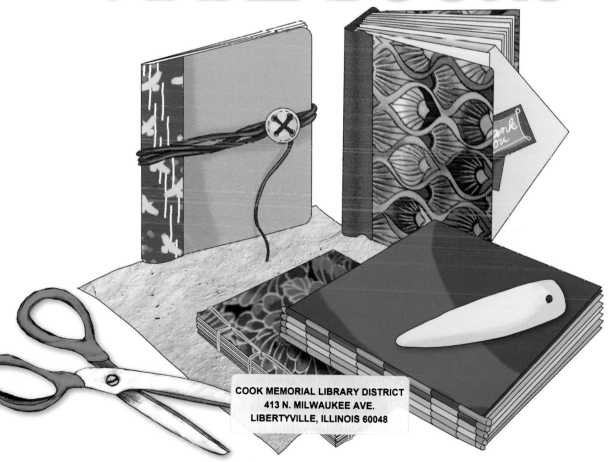

Written and Illustrated by Kathleen Petelinsek

CHERRY LAKE PUBLISHING • ANN ARBOR, MICHIGAN

CHERRY LAKE
Publishing

Published in the United States of America by Cherry Lake Publishing
Ann Arbor, Michigan
www.cherrylakepublishing.com

Photo Credits: Page 4, ©Lucidwaters/Dreamstime.com; page 5, ©alterfalter/Shutterstock; page 6, ©Bozhdb/Dreamstime.com; page 8, ©Kesaree Prakumthong/Dreamstime.com

Library of Congress Cataloging-in-Publication Data
Petelinsek, Kathleen.
 Learning to make books / by Kathleen Petelinsek.
    pages cm
 Includes bibliographical references and index.
 ISBN 978-1-63362-372-9 (lib. bdg.) — ISBN 978-1-63362-400-9 (pbk.) — ISBN 978-1-63362-456-6 (ebook) — ISBN 978-1-63362-428-3 (pdf)
 1. Bookbinding—Juvenile literature. 2. Book design—Juvenile literature. I. Title.
 Z271.P48 2016
 686.3—dc23   2015006483

Cherry Lake Publishing would like to acknowledge the work of the Partnership for 21st Century Skills. Please visit www.p21.org for more information.

Printed in the United States of America
Corporate Graphics
July 2015

TABLE OF CONTENTS

The History of Books

Scrolls did not have pages the way modern books do.

Can you imagine life without books? In ancient times, there was no such thing as paper. People recorded stories on the walls of caves. They also wrote on wood, stones, bones, shells, pottery, and clay tablets.

Eventually, a paperlike material called **papyrus** was invented. People wrote things down on long pieces of papyrus called scrolls. Scrolls were rolled and stored in a container that was labeled with the title or subject. Over time, a material called **parchment**, made from the skins of animals, replaced papyrus.

Paper was invented in China around 105 CE. At about the same time, a type of book called a codex began to replace scrolls. A codex is made from individual sheets of parchment that are stacked together and bound, similar to the books we read today.

As Chinese people exchanged goods with foreign traders, paper began to spread around the world. It eventually became a common, inexpensive product and replaced parchment as the most popular material for making books.

Today's books are printed using machines called printing presses.

The Art of Making a Book

You can decorate your books to create a custom look.

Before the invention of the printing press in 1440, books had to be written by hand. They were rare and valuable works of art. Today, almost all books are mass-produced. However, you can still make your own books using traditional methods. Handmade books can be used to journal, scrapbook, sketch, and put collections of recipes or photos. They also make great gifts for your friends and family!

The process of making a book starts with paper. You can use plain white paper, gift wrap, paper bags, or decorative paper. Once you have chosen the right paper for your book, the next step is to fold and **bind** the pages together. There are many methods of binding books. You can staple, sew, glue, or tape pages together. Covers can be made from paper, cardboard, wood, leather, or other materials.

As you develop your bookbinding skills, keep a box to collect and organize your supplies. This way you will have a wide variety of paper and materials for creating your one-of-a-kind masterpieces.

An electronic book, or e-book, is another form of a book that is popular today.

Basic Tools

You will need to gather some tools and materials before you start making books. You might find some of these items around your house. You can purchase any others at a craft store.

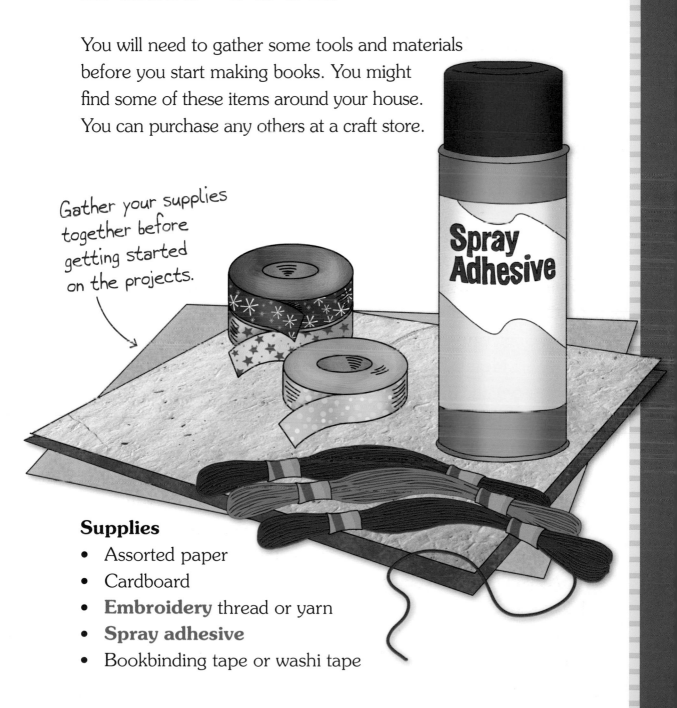

Gather your supplies together before getting started on the projects.

Spray Adhesive

Supplies
- Assorted paper
- Cardboard
- **Embroidery** thread or yarn
- **Spray adhesive**
- Bookbinding tape or washi tape

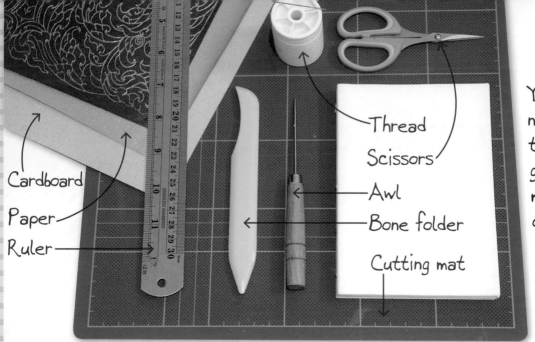

Cardboard

Paper

Ruler

Thread

Scissors

Awl

Bone folder

Cutting mat

You'll only need a few tools to get started making your own books.

Tools

- Awl: Use an awl or another sharp, pointed tool to punch holes through pages. You can make an awl by asking an adult to help you poke the eye of a needle into a cork.
- Bone folder: Use this tool to make sharp creases, **score** lines, or **burnish** papers smooth.
- Ruler: Metal rulers work best for making books.
- Scissors and/or craft knife: If you are using a craft knife, ask an adult to help so you do not cut yourself.
- Long-arm stapler: Stapling pages together is one of the easiest ways to make a book.
- Needle: Choose the right needle based on the thread you are using.
- Glue gun: A glue gun is great for gluing heavier materials together. Ask an adult to help you use this tool.
- Binder clips: These are helpful for holding the pages of your book together before you bind them.
- Cutting mat: Use this tool to protect your work surface.

Stitches and Knots

The projects in this book require you to do some basic stitching. Sharpen your skills by practicing on a piece of scrap cloth or paper before you stitch your project.

Materials
- Embroidery thread
- Embroidery needle
- Scrap felt or paper
- Scissors

Threading a Needle
1. Cut a 36-inch (91 centimeters) length of thread.
2. Insert the thread through the eye of the needle. To do this, hold the needle between your thumb and forefinger, and poke the thread through the eye.
3. Pull the thread until it is halfway through the needle's eye. Tie the loose ends together.

Running Stitch

1. Poke the threaded needle from the back side of the fabric up through the front. Pull the thread all the way through the fabric.
2. Poke the needle back through the front of the fabric next to where it poked out from the bottom. Pull the thread through. You have created your first stitch!
3. Repeat, leaving a small space between each stitch.

Knot

1. Once you are done stitching, you need to tie a knot to keep the stitches from coming apart.
2. On the back side of your fabric, form a loop in the thread. Now put the needle through the loop. This will create the beginning of your knot.
3. As you pull the thread through the loop, guide the knot down toward the fabric. You want the knot to lie right next to the last stitch in the fabric. Pull the knot tight.

Simple Paper Bag Book

This book is great for sketching pictures of the things you see while out on a hike. It is small enough to slip into your pocket.

Materials

- 5 sheets of white paper, 8.5 inches (21.6 cm) by 11 inches (28 cm)
- Ruler
- Pencil
- Scissors
- Bone folder
- Brown paper bag
- Binder clips
- Long-arm stapler
- Watercolors

Steps

1. Measure and cut the sheets of white paper in half crosswise so you have 10 sheets of paper measuring 8.5 inches (21.6 cm) by 5.5 inches (14 cm). These will be the pages to your book.
2. Fold each sheet in half crosswise. When the paper is folded, it will measure 4.25 inches (10.8 cm) by 5.5 inches (14 cm).

4.25"

5.5"

Crease each fold with the bone folder and set them aside.

3. Measure and cut a rectangle from the brown paper bag that measures 9 inches (23 cm) by 6 inches (15 cm). This will be the cover of your book.

4. Fold the rectangle exactly in half crosswise. Crease it using the bone folder. The size of the folded bag should be 4.5 inches (11.4 cm) by 6 inches (15 cm).

5. Open up all the folded sheets of white paper. Lay the brown bag rectangle on your work surface. Stack the sheets of white paper evenly on top of it. Line up all the corners and creases of the white sheets. Center them in the crease of the brown bag. Once everything is in place, clip the pages and cover together using the binder clips.

6. Turn the stack of clipped papers upside down so the brown bag is on top. Carefully staple the book in three spots along the crease using a long-arm stapler.

7. Remove the binder clips.

8. Use your watercolors, brush, and water to decorate your book's cover.

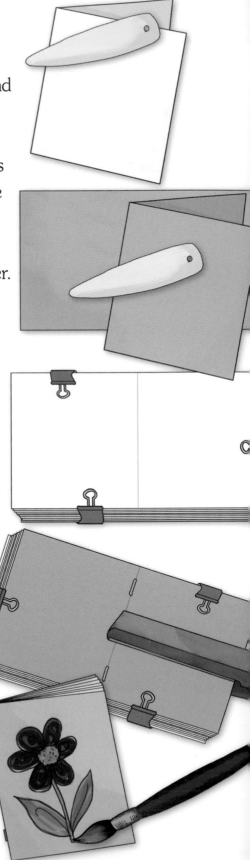

Button Up!

This little book is great for keeping a private journal of your thoughts. Keep your secrets safe by buttoning up your journal.

Materials

- 5 sheets of white paper, 8.5 inches (21.6 cm) by 11 inches (28 cm)
- Sheet of decorative paper, 9 inches (23 cm) by 12 inches (30.5 cm)
- Ruler
- Pencil
- Scissors
- Cardboard from a cereal box, 9 inches (15 cm) by 12 inches (30.5 cm)
- Bone folder
- Spray adhesive
- Binder clips
- Cutting mat
- Awl
- Embroidery thread
- Embroidery needle
- Large, flat button

TIP: Set up a spray booth using an old box and newspapers. This will keep the spray adhesive from getting all over your work area.

Spray Adhesive

Steps

1. Begin by following steps 1 and 2 on pages 11–12.
2. Cut the decorative paper in half crosswise. You should have two sheets of decorative paper measuring 9 inches (23 cm) by 6 inches (15 cm). Fold them in half to be 4.5 inches (11.4 cm) by 6 inches (15 cm).

3. Place the cereal box rectangle on your work surface, printed side up. Measure and mark a line in the middle, 4.5 inches (11.4 cm) from each side. Score the cardboard along this line using your ruler and bone folder. This will make folding it easier. Once the cardboard is scored, fold it in half and use the bone folder to crease it.

4. Ask an adult to help you spray adhesive on the back side of one decorative sheet of paper. Press it to the printed side of the cereal box. This will be your book's inside cover.

5. Open up the cover so the brown side is lying on the table and the decorative paper is facing up. Open up the folded white sheets of paper and stack them on top. Line them up along the center crease. Clip everything together with the binder clips.

6. Place the clipped papers on the cutting mat. Measure and mark along the crease of the top white sheet of paper every 0.5 inches (1.3 cm). Ask an adult to help

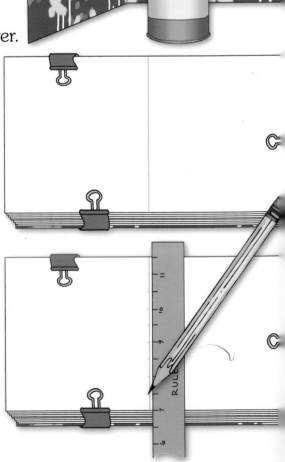

you pierce holes at each mark using the awl. You should have 8 holes along the crease of your stack of papers.

7. Thread your needle. Begin stitching your book together, starting in the inside center of the book. Poke your needle through the center hole and pull the thread through.

8. Poke the needle back through the hole above where your thread came from. Use a running stitch to continue going in and out of the holes above your starting point. Once you have poked the needle through the last hole, wrap the thread around the top of the book and poke the needle back through the last hole you came from.

9. Continue the running stitch all the way down the spine to the other end of the book. When you reach the last hole, wrap the thread around the bottom of the book and stitch back up through the holes.

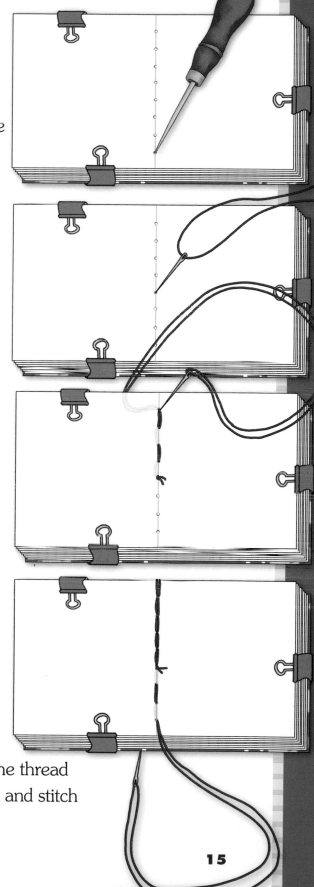

10. This time, stop where you began stitching in the center of the book. Do not knot or cut the thread. Leave your needle threaded and dangling from the inside center of your book. Remove the binder clips.

11. Place the other folded piece of decorative paper on your work surface. Measure 1 inch (2.5 cm) from the fold and mark a line **parallel** to the fold. Cut the paper along this line. Open, the new size should be 2 inches (5 cm) by 5.5 inches (14 cm). Folded, it is 1 inch (2.5 cm) by 5.5 inches (14 cm).

12. Ask an adult to help you spray adhesive to the decorative sheet. Attach it to the stitched edge of the book, covering up the stitching along the outside.

13. Poke the needle you left dangling back through the next hole in the crease, this time pushing it all the way through the decorative sheet of paper you just glued to the book. Knot the thread next to the binding. Cut one of the pieces of thread near the knot. You should now have one long piece of thread hanging.

14. Rethread the needle with a separate piece of thread and sew a button to the front center edge of the book.

15. Wrap the long piece of thread around your book to keep it closed. Secure the thread by wrapping it around the button a few times.

Japanese Stab Binding

Japanese stab binding is a decorative way to stitch together single sheets of paper. This project uses a stitching process called *yotsume toji*, or "four-eye binding."

Materials

- 21 sheets of white paper, 5 inches (12.7 cm) square
- 2 sheets of decorative paper, 5 inches (12.7 cm) square
- Binder clips
- Ruler
- Pencil
- Cutting mat
- Awl
- Embroidery thread
- Embroidery needle

Steps

1. Place one sheet of white paper on your work surface. Use your ruler to measure and draw a parallel line 0.5 inches (1.3 cm) from one side of the paper. Mark the line every inch with a small mark. You should have four evenly spaced marks on the line.

2. Starting at the bottom edge, number each of the marks going upward. This page will be used as the **template** for sewing and binding your book. It will be torn off and thrown away when you are done sewing.

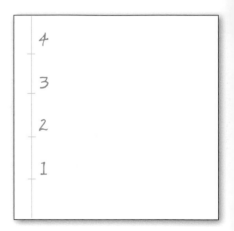

3. Stack the remaining pages of your book together so the decorative papers are on the top and bottom of the stack. Place your template on top of the stack. Clip everything together with a binder clip to hold it in place.

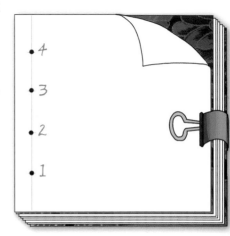

4. Place the stack of papers on the cutting mat. With the help of adult, pierce each of the four marks on your template through the entire stack using the awl.

5. Thread your needle. Begin stitching by poking the threaded needle through hole 2 on the back cover. Pull the thread up through the front of the stack.

6. Wrap the thread around the spine and once again send it back through hole 2 from the back to the front.

7. From the front of hole 2, send the needle down through hole 1. The needle will end on the back cover of hole 1.

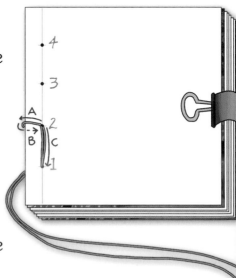

8. Wrap the thread around the spine and send it back through the front of hole 1.

9. Wrap the thread around the bottom of the book and again go through hole 1 from the front of the book.

10. From the back side, poke the needle through hole 2.

11. From the front of the book, go through hole 3.

12. From the back side, go through hole 4.

13. Wrap the thread around the spine. Send the needle through the back of hole 4 to the front.

14. Wrap the thread around the top edge of the book. Go through the back of hole 4, again ending in the front.

15. Send the needle through hole 3 from the front to the back.

16. Wrap the thread around the spine and back through the front of hole 3.

17. Tie a knot in the thread at the back side of the book. Trim the loose ends of thread.

18. Remove the binder clip and gently rip the template from the front cover. Be careful not to tear any of the other sheets.

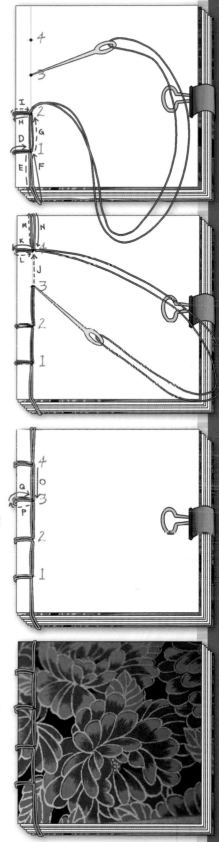

Piano Hinged Book

This simple and unique binding method will give your book a distinctive appearance.

Materials

- 6 pieces of scrapbook paper, 6 inches (15 cm) by 12 inches (30.5 cm)
- Ruler
- Bone folder
- Pencil
- Scissors
- 7 bamboo skewers
- Saw

Steps

1. Fold each of the 6 scrapbook pages in half crosswise so they measure 6 inches by 6 inches (15 by 15 cm).

2. Use your ruler to measure 0.25 inches (0.64 cm) from each side of the crease on one folded scrapbook page. Use your bone folder to score two lines at these points and parallel to the crease.

3. Use your ruler and pencil to make marks every 0.5 inches (1.3 cm) along the folded edge of the paper.

4. Use your scissors to snip each of the marks from the fold to the score lines.
5. Starting at the top, fold every other snip forward. Repeat steps 2 through 5 with the remaining 5 sheets of paper.
6. Stack two of the pages together. Run a bamboo skewer through the first notch of the bottom sheet of paper and through the second notch of the top page. Next send the skewer through the third notch of the bottom page and the fourth notch of the top page. Continue sending the skewer through the tabs, threading them together.
7. Fold back the tabs that were folded in on the second sheet and place a third sheet of paper on top of the two you just threaded. Connect the second and third sheets of paper with a bamboo skewer using the same method you used to connect the first two.
8. Continue until you have connected all six sheets together.
9. The front and back pages will have empty notches every other notch. Thread a bamboo skewer through these notches as well.
10. Ask an adult to help you cut off the loose ends of the bamboo skewers with the saw.

Envelope Scrapbook

Keep mementos such as concert tickets, photos, postcards, and letters in this unique envelope book. This project is made with a soft cover. You can also make it with a hardbound cover (see pages 25–28).

Materials

- 8 to 12 envelopes, all the same size
- Piece of heavyweight decorative paper that is at least twice the size of an envelope
- Scissors
- Ruler
- Pencil
- Bone folder
- Bookbinding tape or washi tape, 0.5 inches (1.3 cm) wide

Steps

1. Determine the size of your book's cover by measuring an envelope. Measure the width of your envelope, multiply that times 4, and add 0.5 inches (1.3 cm). That's the length of your cover. The cover's height should be 0.5 inches (1.3 cm) taller than the height of the envelope. For example, if an

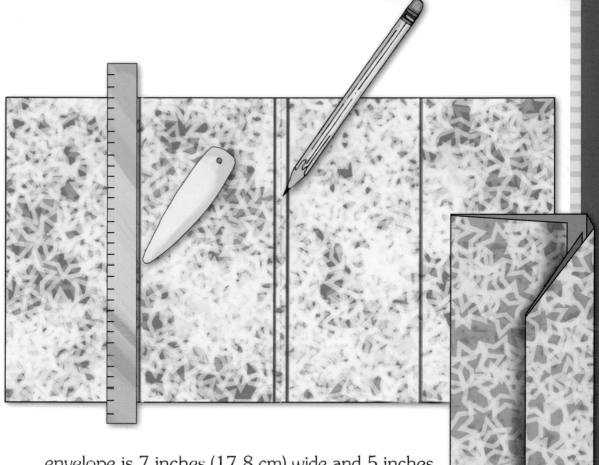

envelope is 7 inches (17.8 cm) wide and 5 inches (12.7 cm) tall, your cover would be 28.5 inches (72.4 cm) long and 5.5 inches (14 cm) tall.

2. Use your ruler and pencil to measure and lightly mark the center of your cover. Using your bone folder and ruler, score a crease on either side of the center point from top to bottom. The creases should be parallel and 0.25 inches (0.64 cm) apart. Fold inward along the creases. Sharpen the folds with your bone folder.

3. Lie the cover flat again. From each crease, measure out the height of an envelope plus 0.25 inches (0.64 cm). Score a crease parallel to the center crease on both marks. Fold inward along these creases. Sharpen the creases with your bone folder. Set the cover aside.

One envelope faces up, one faces down.

4. To bind your envelopes, lay two envelopes side by side with the bottoms touching. Tape the bottoms of the envelopes together. Flip the right-hand envelope onto the left-hand envelope, as you would a page in a book. Lay a third envelope to the right of the flipped envelope. Again, the bottoms of the envelopes should touch. Tape the bottoms together. Turn that envelope over. Continue taping the bottoms of all the envelopes together. Trim away any excess tape.

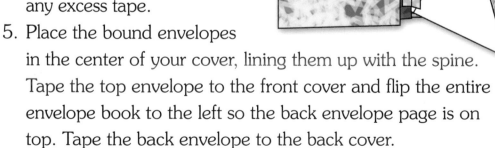

5. Place the bound envelopes in the center of your cover, lining them up with the spine. Tape the top envelope to the front cover and flip the entire envelope book to the left so the back envelope page is on top. Tape the back envelope to the back cover.

6. Fold the front and back panels of the cover inward to complete the book.

Hardbound Cover

You can attach this hard cover to any of the projects in this book. It is especially nice for the Envelope Scrapbook (page 22).

Materials

- Mat board
- Cutting mat
- Ruler
- Craft knife
- Decorative paper
- Pencil
- Bone folder
- Spray adhesive
- Duct tape
- Ribbon
- Plain paper for book lining
- Glue gun
- Binder clips

Ask an adult to help cut the mat board.

Steps

1. Measure the height, width, and thickness of your book. This will determine the size of the cover.
2. You will need 2 pieces of mat board for the front and back covers. Each piece should be 0.25 inches (0.64 cm) taller than your book and 0.5 inches (1.3 cm) less wide than your book. To cut the mat board, place your ruler along the line you wish to cut. Gently run the craft knife along the edge of the ruler to score the board. Do not try to cut all the way through the board in one pass. Instead, make several passes with the knife to make one cut.

0.5" less wide

0.25" taller

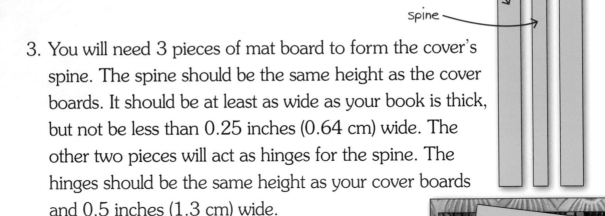

hinges

spine

3. You will need 3 pieces of mat board to form the cover's spine. The spine should be the same height as the cover boards. It should be at least as wide as your book is thick, but not be less than 0.25 inches (0.64 cm) wide. The other two pieces will act as hinges for the spine. The hinges should be the same height as your cover boards and 0.5 inches (1.3 cm) wide.

4. Next, you will need 2 pieces of decorative paper that are 1 inch (2.5 cm) longer and wider than the front and back covers. Cut the paper to size.

5. Lay one piece of the decorative paper (decorated side down) on the table. Center a cover board on top of it. Trace around the mat board with your pencil. Remove the board and score the pencil lines with your bone folder and ruler.

6. Cut the corners from the sheet of paper.

7. Ask an adult to help you spray the back side of the decorative paper with adhesive.

8. Set the sprayed paper adhesive side up. Place the front cover on the adhesive, centering it in the lines you traced. Wrap the 0.5-inch (1.3 cm) edges around the mat board. Burnish the paper to the mat board using your bone folder.

9. Repeat steps 5 through 7 to cover the back mat board.

Set up an adhesive spray booth using an old box.

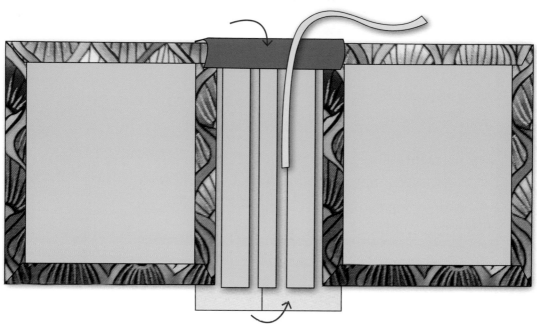

10. Cut 2 pieces of duct tape that are 2 inches (5 cm) longer than the height of your mat board pieces. Lay them, adhesive side up, with one overlapping the other slightly. (If your book has a wide spine, you may need to use a third piece of duct tape.)

11. Lay the spine mat board in the center of the pieces of tape. Lay the hinge mat boards on either side of the spine. Leave a 0.125 inch (0.317 cm) gap between each piece.

12. Lay the front and back covers next to the hinged pieces with their back sides facing up. Again, leave a 0.125-inch (0.317 cm) gap between the pieces. Make sure all the pieces of mat board line up along their top and bottom sides. Gently press them down to stick them to the tape.

13. Wrap the top of the tape over the top of the cover. Do the same at the bottom.

14. Cut a ribbon that is the height of your book. Place it halfway up the spine. Let the other half extend over the top of the book.

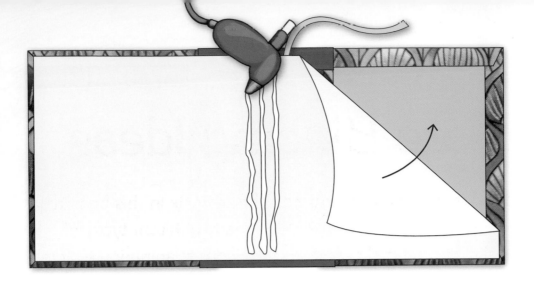

15. Measure the height and width of your unfolded cover. The lining paper should be 0.25 inches (0.64 cm) smaller than your overall cover size in both height and width. Cut the lining paper to size. Ask an adult to help you spray the lining paper with adhesive in your spray booth.

16. Carefully lay the lining paper on the inside of your book cover (and ribbon). Make sure about 0.125 inches (0.317 cm) of the cover are showing on each side of the lining. Burnish using your bone folder. The ribbon should be sandwiched between the lining paper and cover.

17. To glue your book to your cover, use a glue gun to apply a generous amount of glue to the spine and hinges of the inside cover. Lay the book down on the back cover, with the sewn edge lining up with the back hinge and spine. Wrap the cover around the book, pressing the spine and front hinge to the book as you go. Clamp the binder clips to the spine and allow it to dry. Remove the clips and enjoy your new hardbound book!

More Binding Ideas

Bookbinding is an ancient art. The projects in this book have only scratched the surface of the many different types of books you can make. Can you use your imagination to think of other creative ways to bind a book? What if you use paper, wood, a drill, and screws? How about paper, a three-hole punch, and a stick from a tree?

Now that you have made a few books, carry one of them around with you to use as a journal. Sketch your new book project ideas in its pages. Make sure your sketchbook is handy at all times so you can draw an idea the instant you think of it. What will you make next?

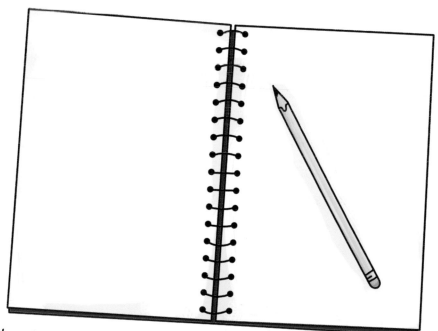

What ideas will you have for making new handmade books?

Glossary

bind (BINDE) to fasten a book's pages together between covers

burnish (BUR-nish) to make something smooth by rubbing it with a tool

embroidery (em-BROI-duh-ree) having to do with the art of sewing a picture or a design onto cloth using different colors of thread or yarn

papyrus (puh-PYE-rus) paperlike material made from the stems of tall water plants that grow in northern Africa and southern Europe

parallel (PAR-uh-lel) staying the same distance from each other and never crossing or meeting

parchment (PAHRCH-muhnt) heavy sheets of paperlike material made from the skin of sheep, goats, or other animals

score (SKOR) to mark the surface of something with cuts, scratches, notches, or lines

spray adhesive (SPRAY ad-HEE-siv) a substance, such as glue, that makes things stick together

template (TEM-plit) a shape or pattern that you draw or cut around to make the same shape in another material

For More Information

Books

Diehn, Gwen. *Journal Your Way: Designing & Using Handmade Books*. Asheville, NC: Lark Crafts, 2013.

Petelinsek, Kathleen. *Learning to Sew*. Ann Arbor, MI: Cherry Lake Publishing, 2014.

Yomtov, Nel. *How to Write a Comic Book*. Ann Arbor, MI: Cherry Lake Publishing, 2013.

Web Sites

Craft x Stew: How to Bind a Book

http://craftstew.com/bookbinding/how-to-bind-a-book

Find links to more than 100 project ideas, from creating new and different books to recycling old ones.

Scholastic Story Starters Adventure

www.scholastic.com/teachers/story-starters/

Do you want to write a story and need ideas? Check out this Web site.

Index

About the Author

Kathleen Petelinsek is a children's book author, illustrator, and designer. As a child, she spent her summers drawing and painting. She still loves to do the same today, but now all her artwork is done on the computer. When she isn't working on her computer, she can be found outside swimming, biking, running, or playing in the Minnesota snow.